Reptiles

COLORING BOOK FOR KIDS!

A Unique Collection Of Coloring Pages

Bold Illustrations
COLORING BOOKS

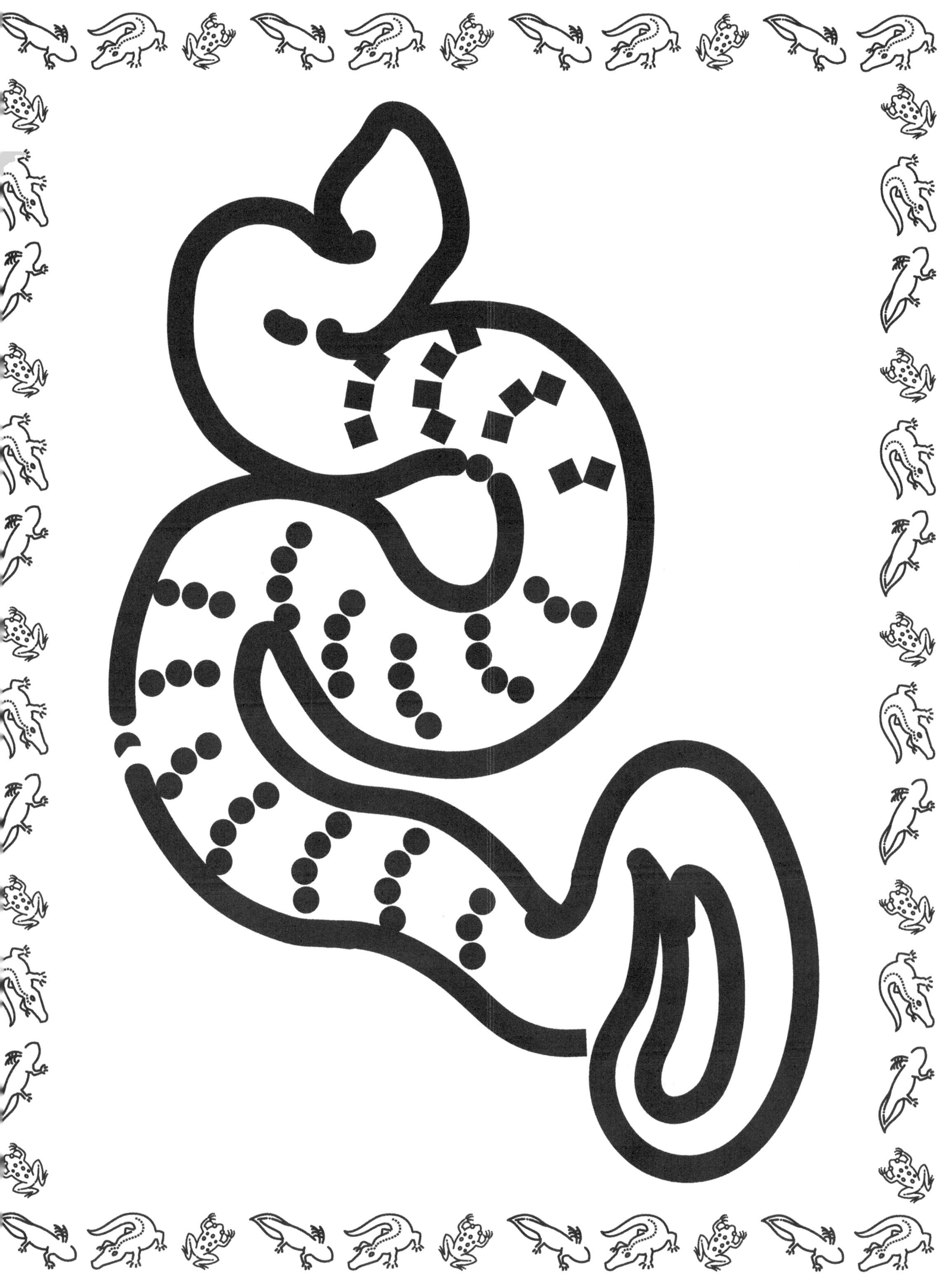

This is a Bleed Through Page If You Are Using a Colouring Marker or Pen!

Find Other Great Titles By searching for Bold Illustrations on Your Favorite Book Retailer

Amazon.Ca | Barnes & Noble (BN.Com) | Books A Million (BAM.Com)

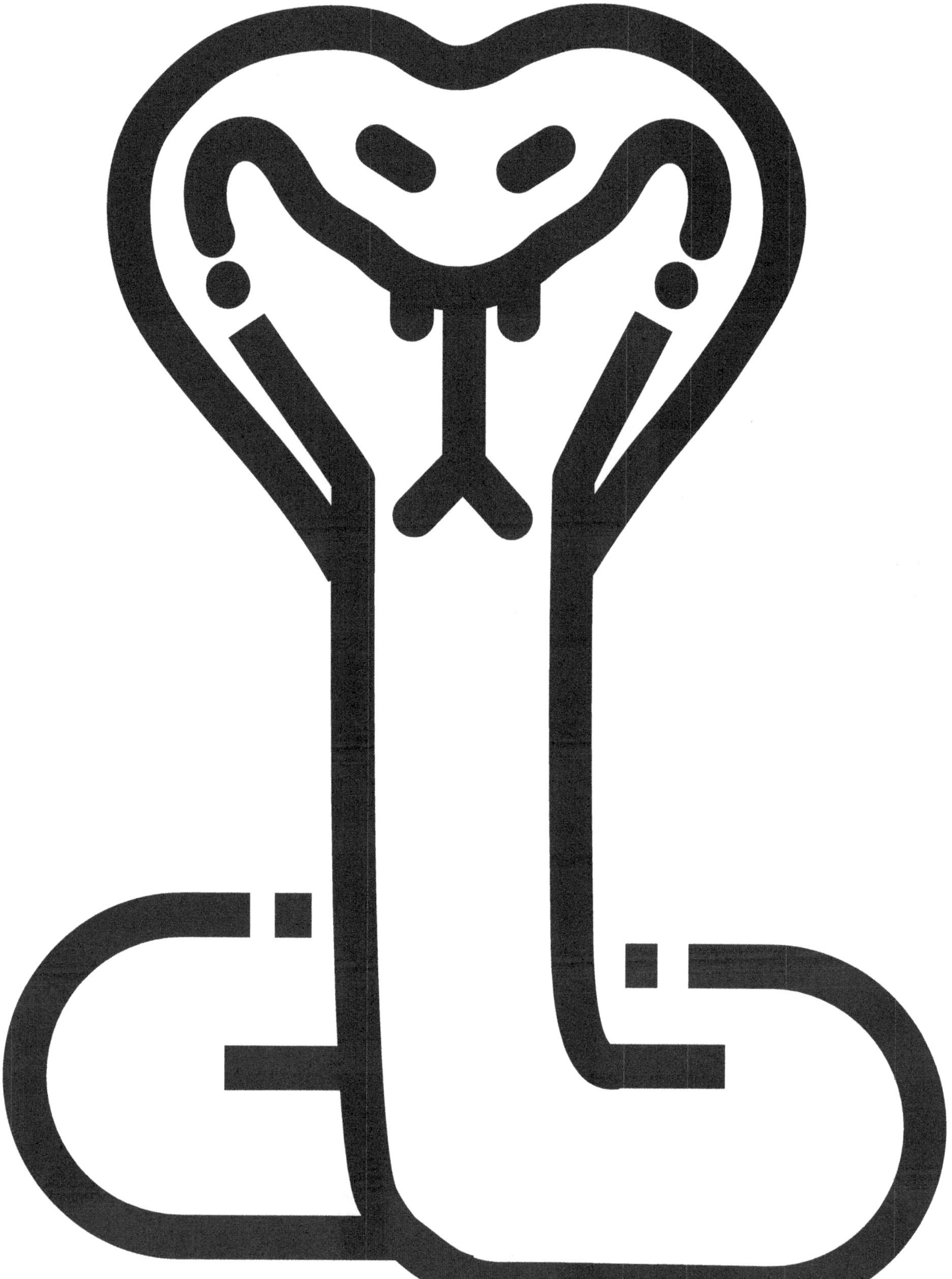

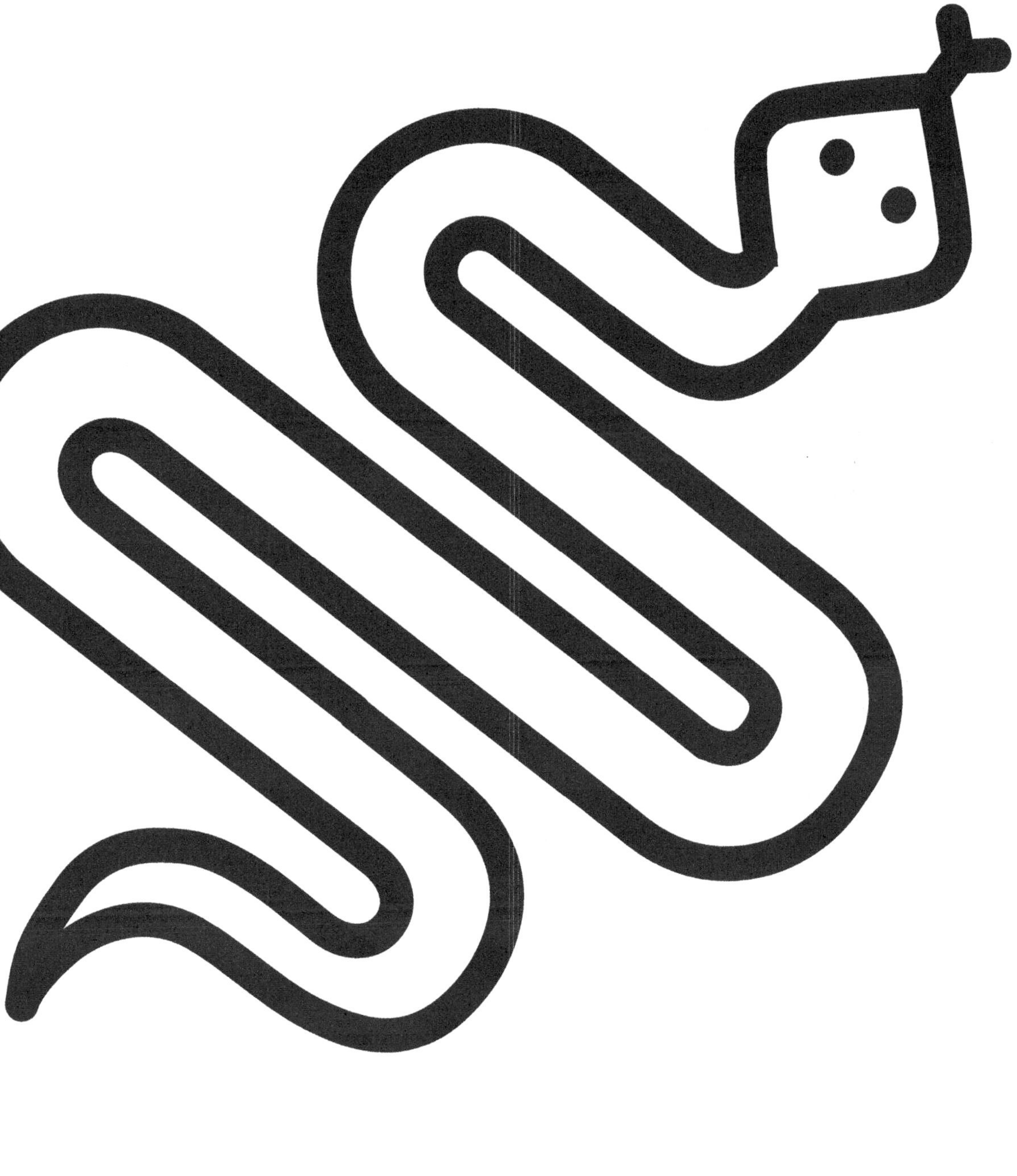

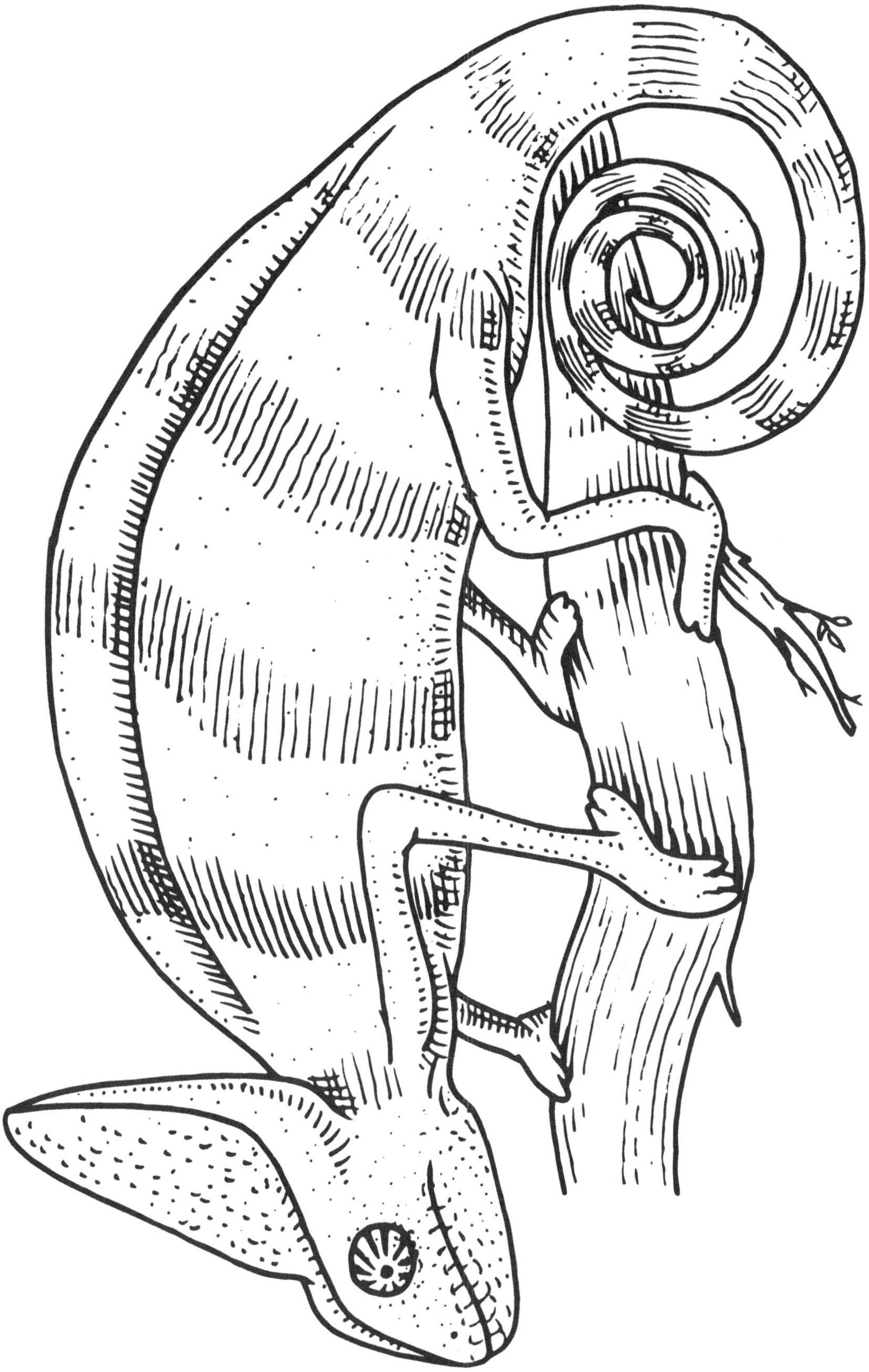

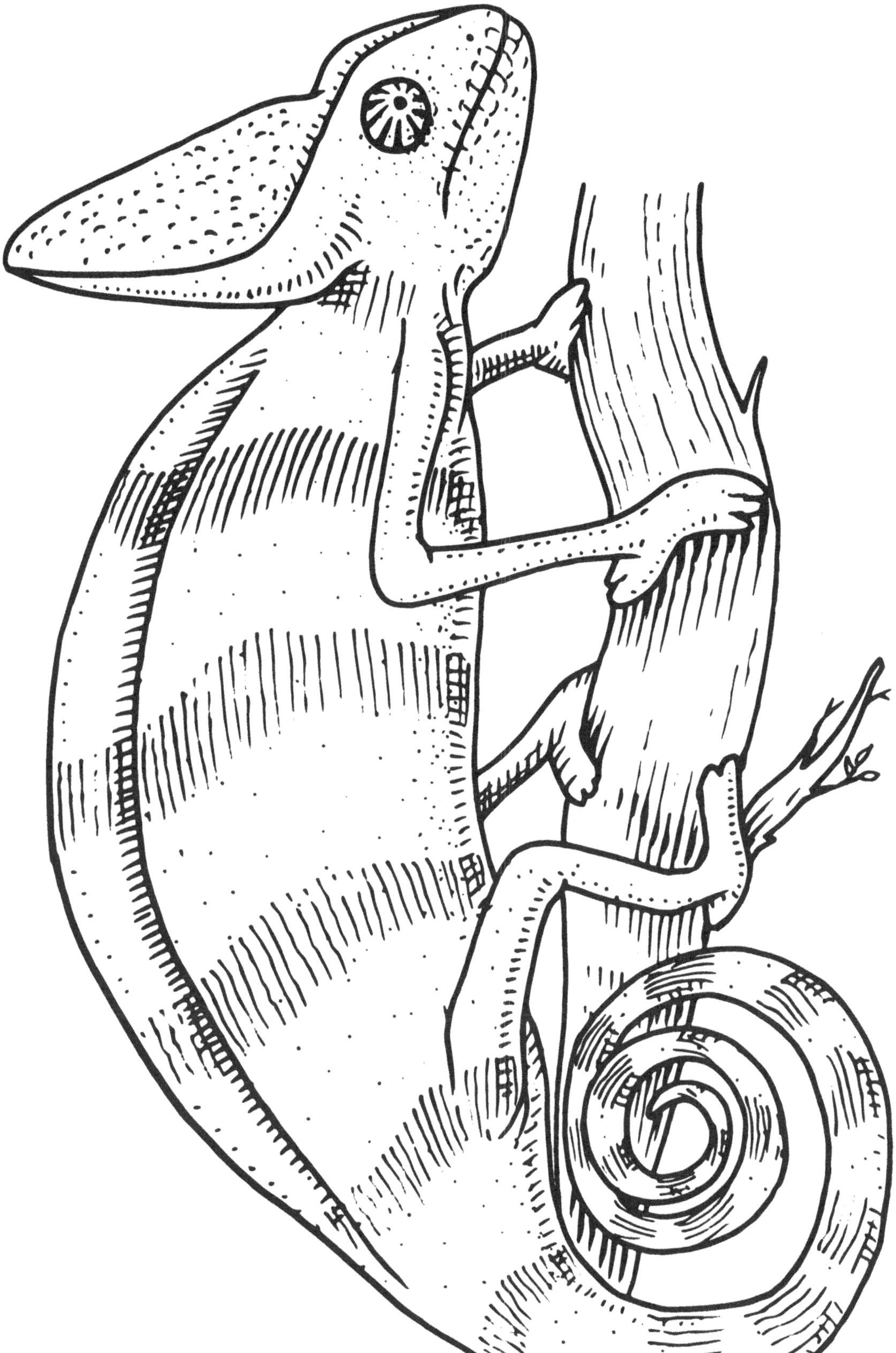

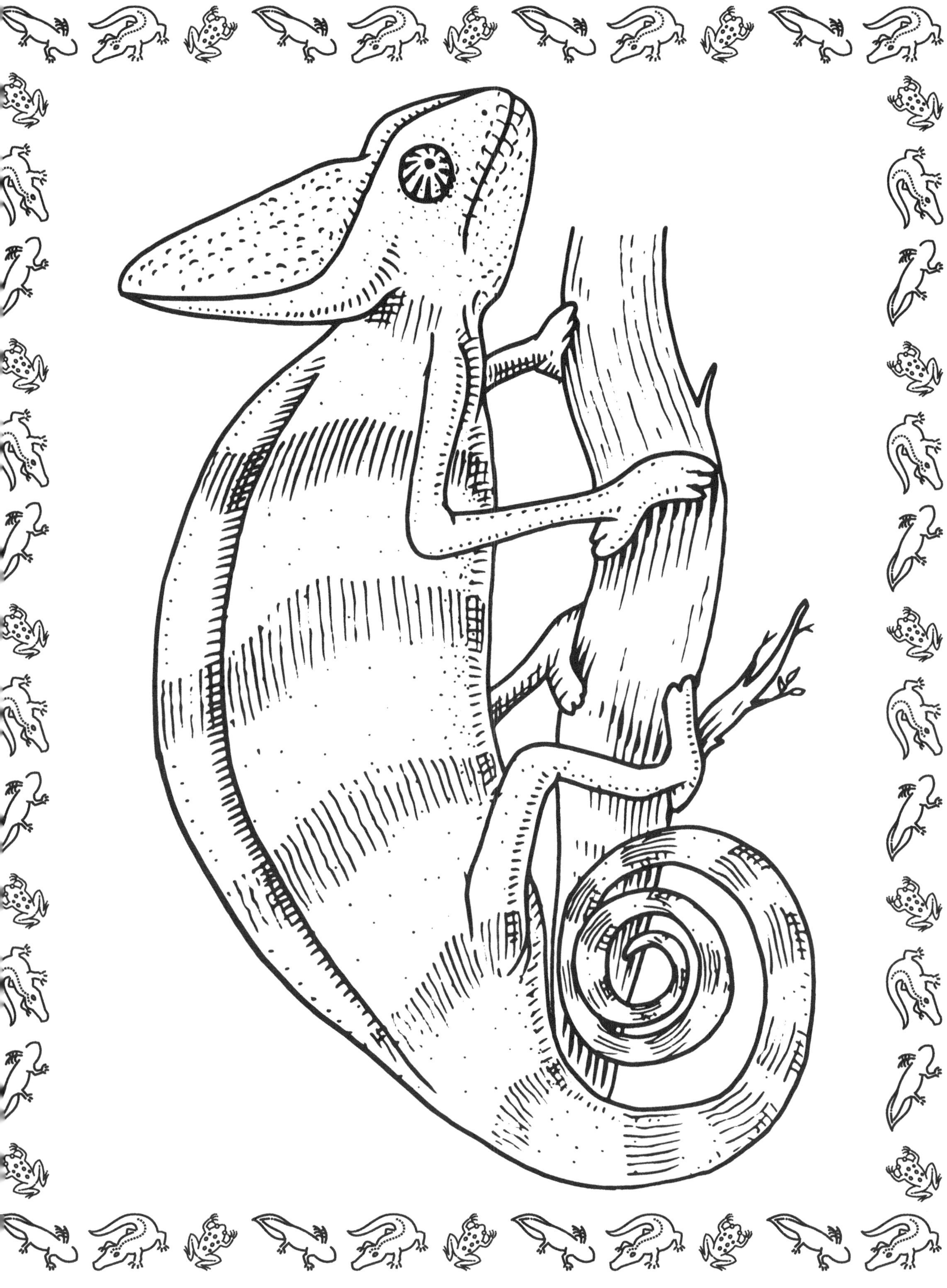

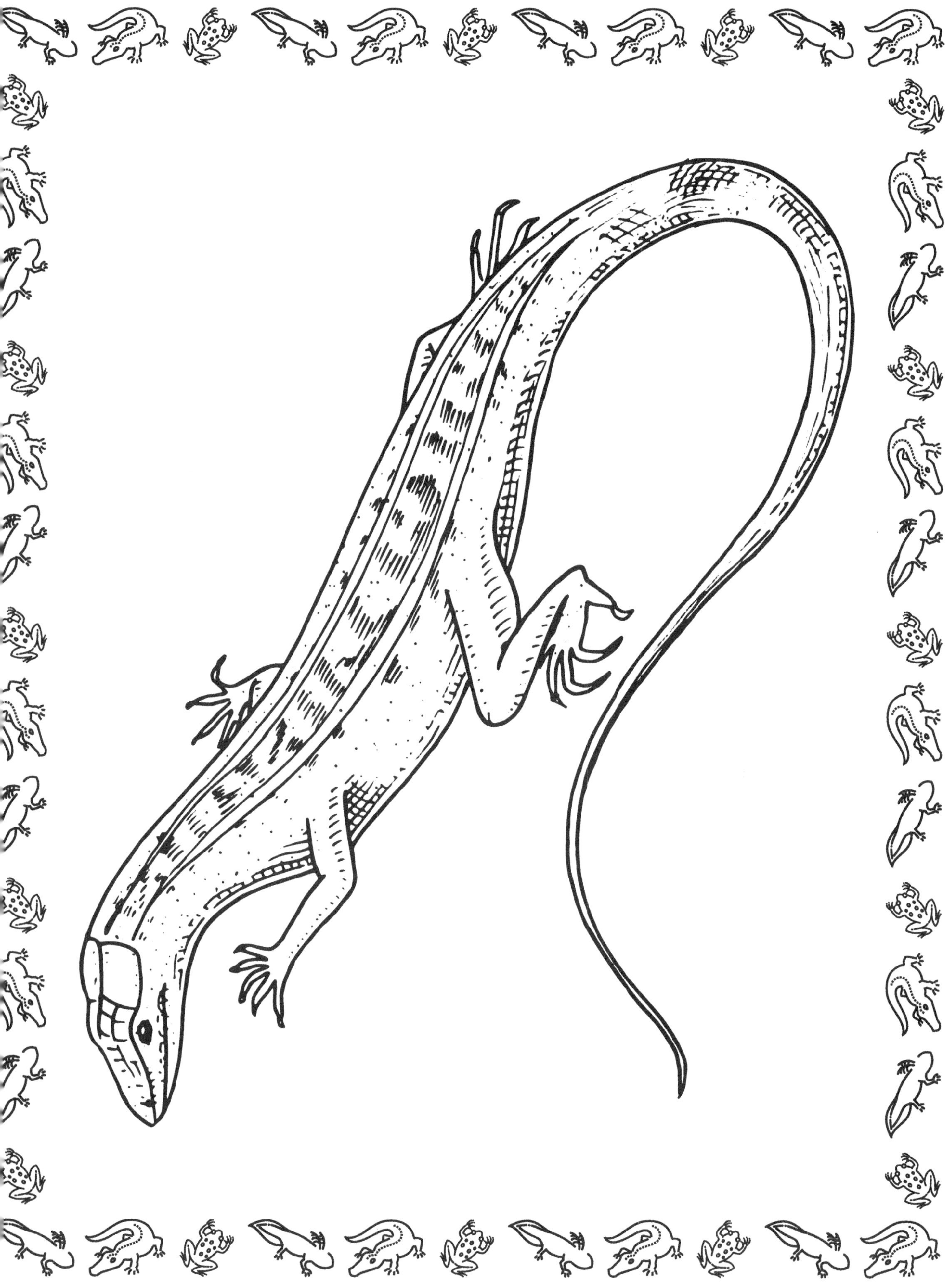

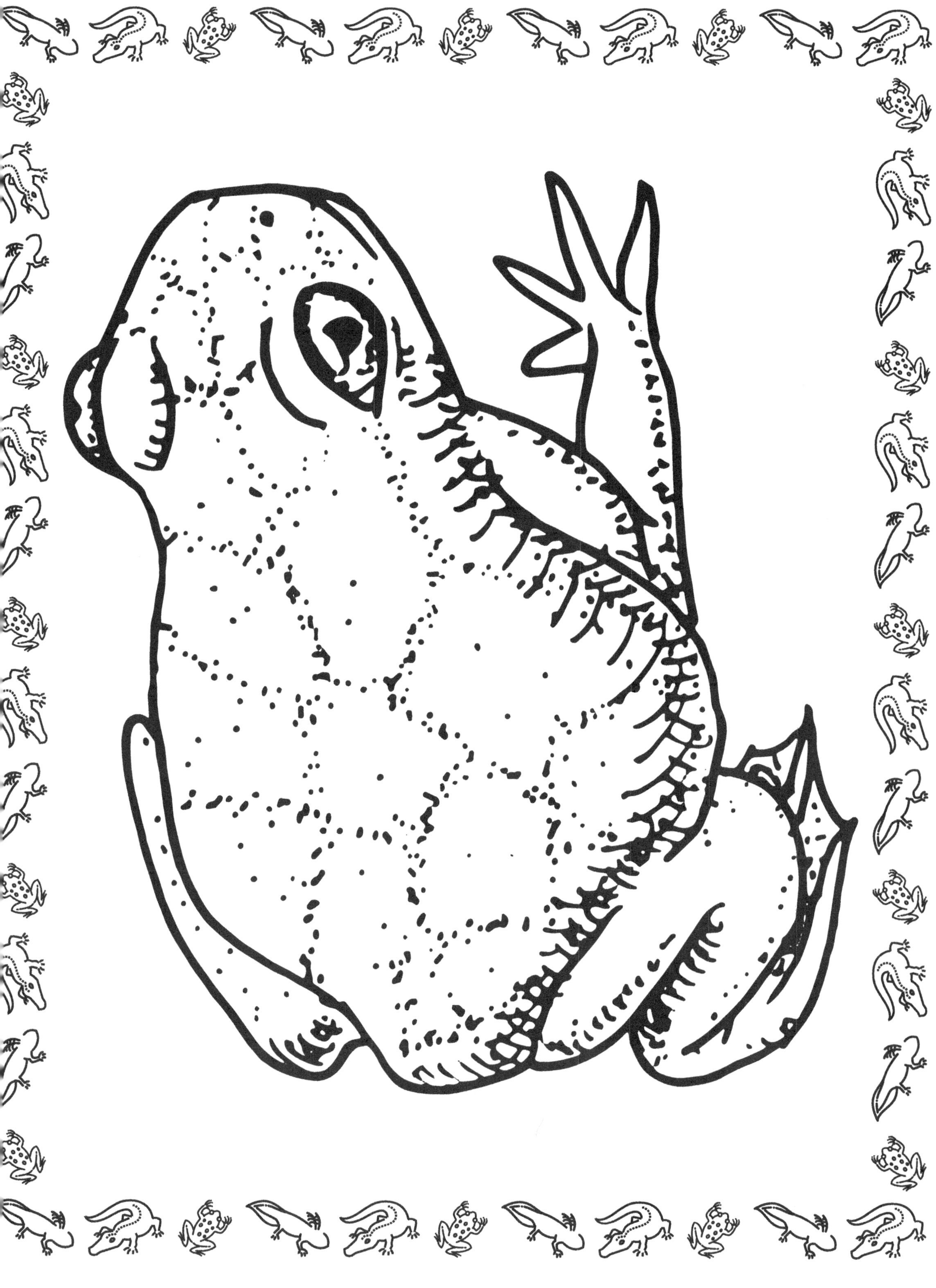

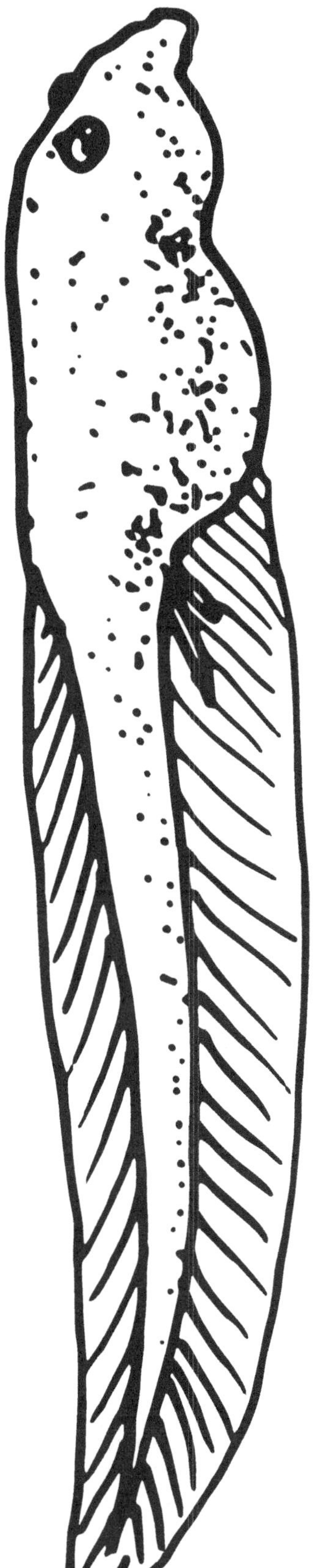

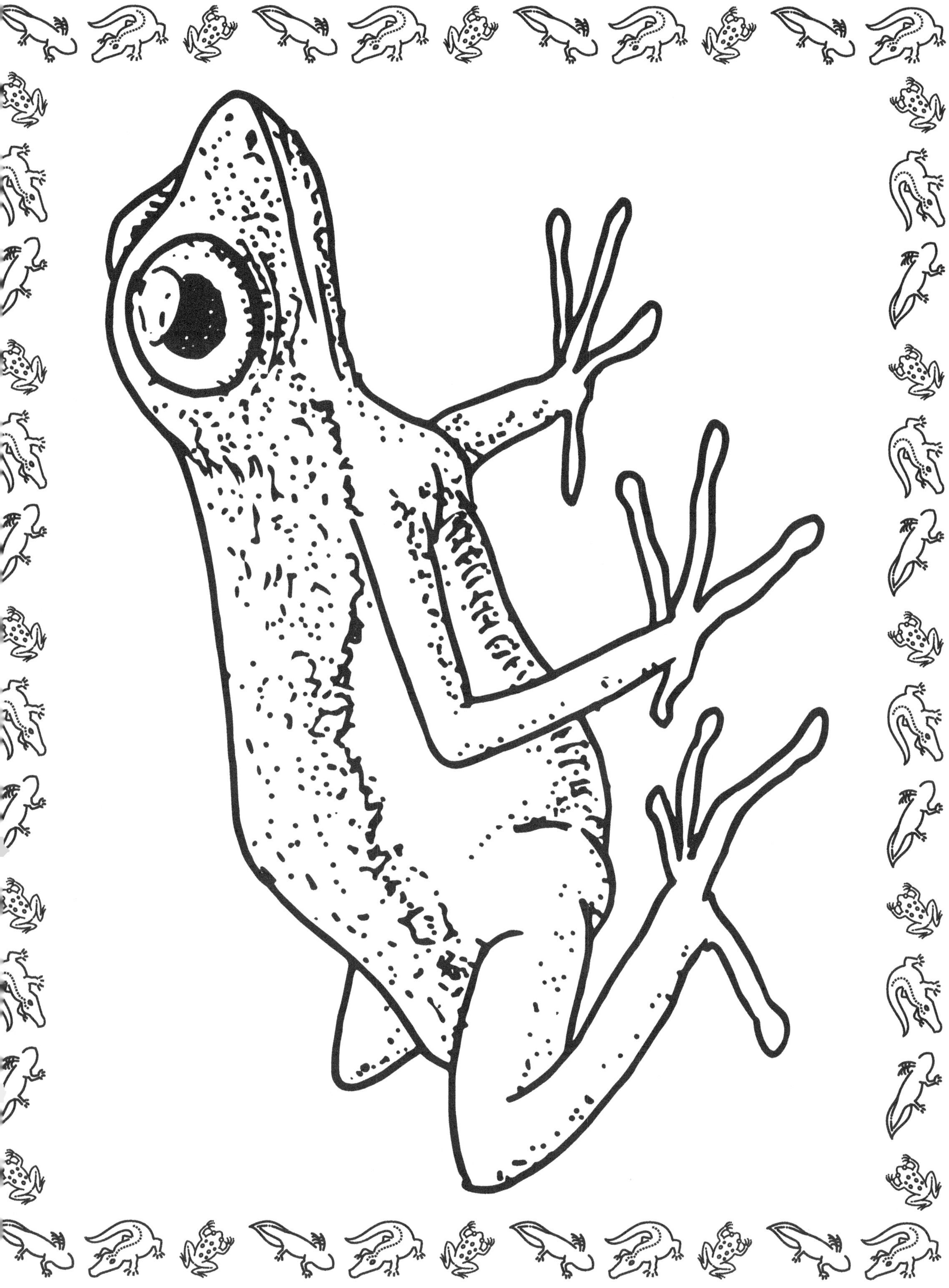

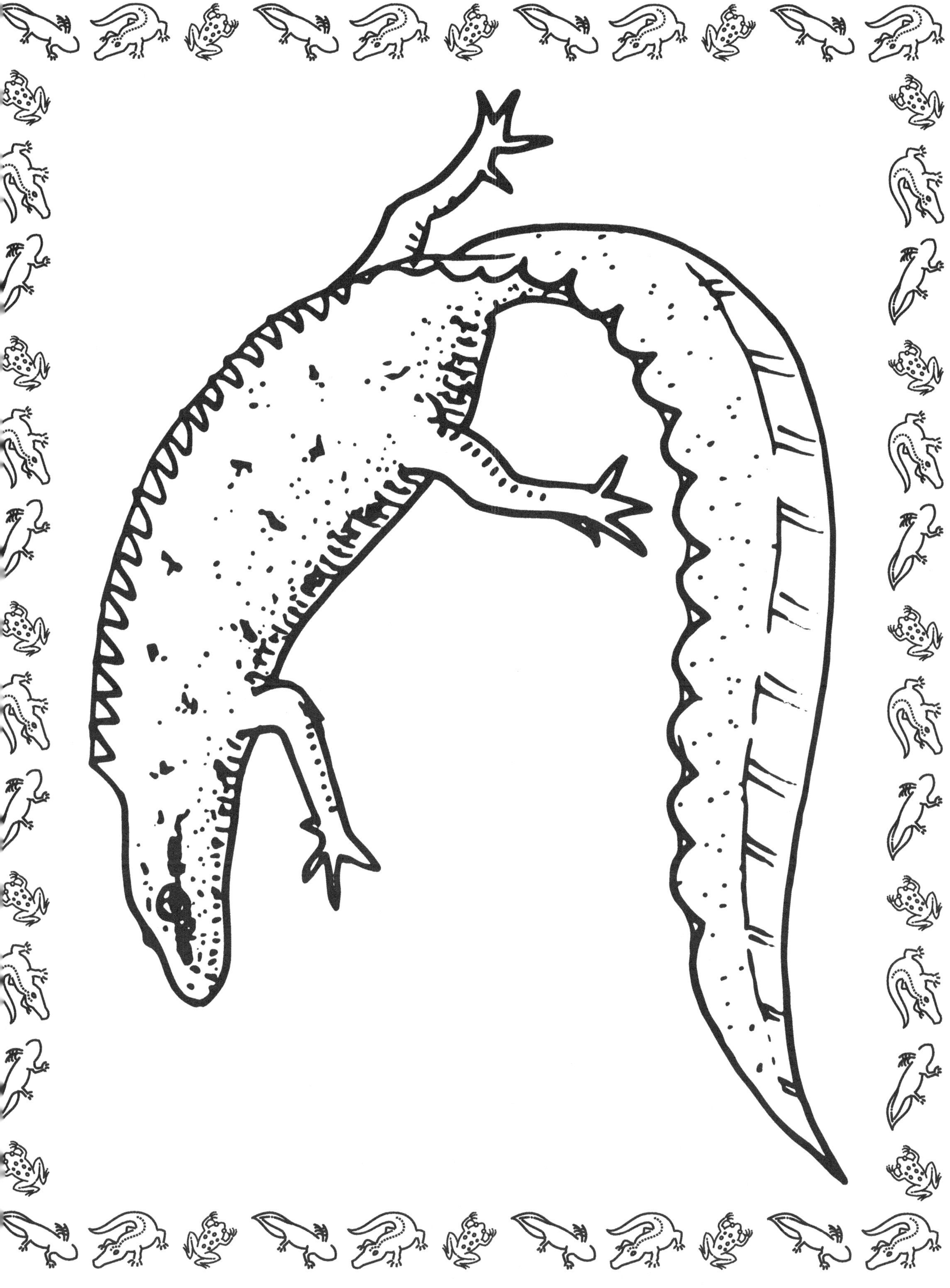

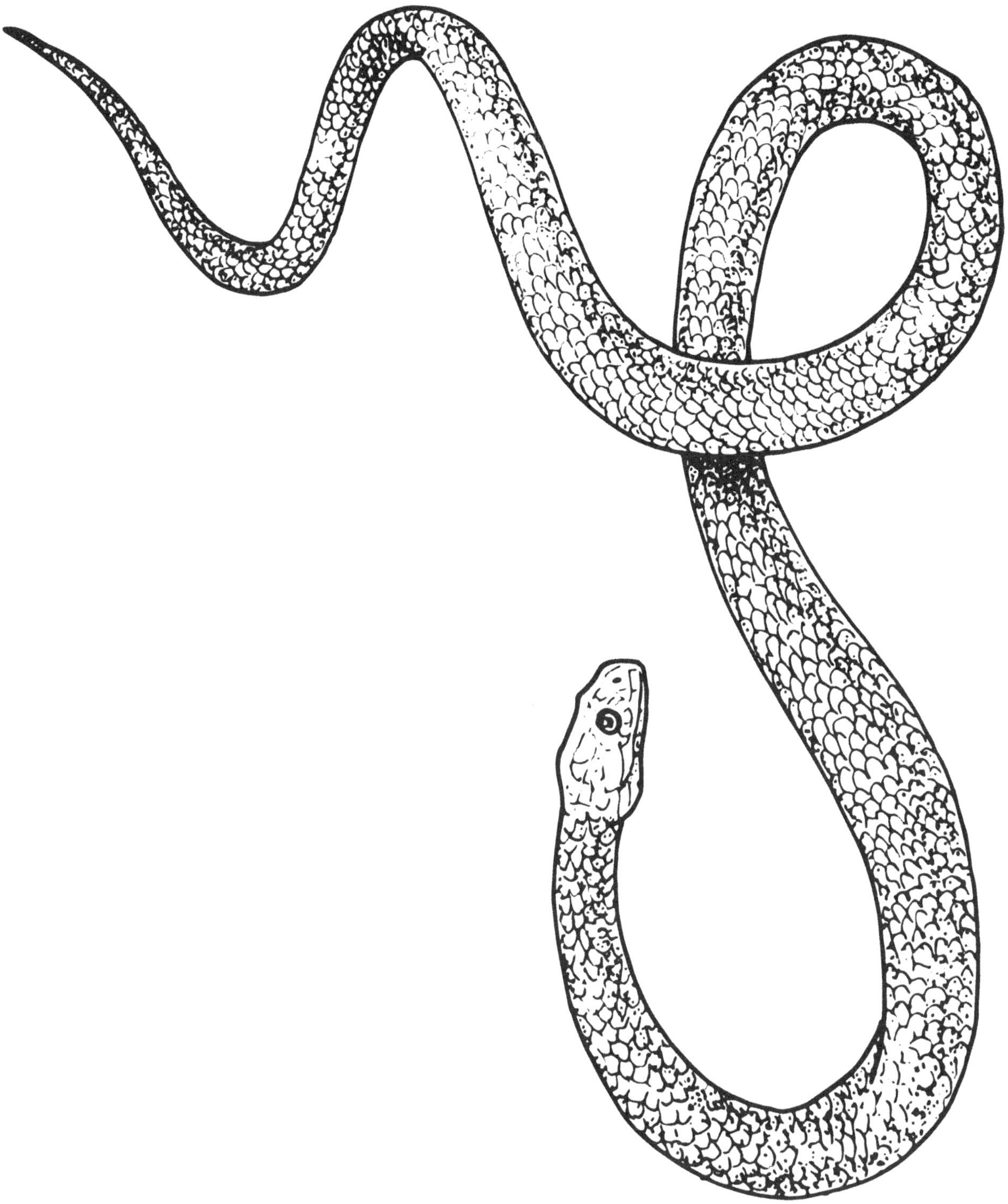

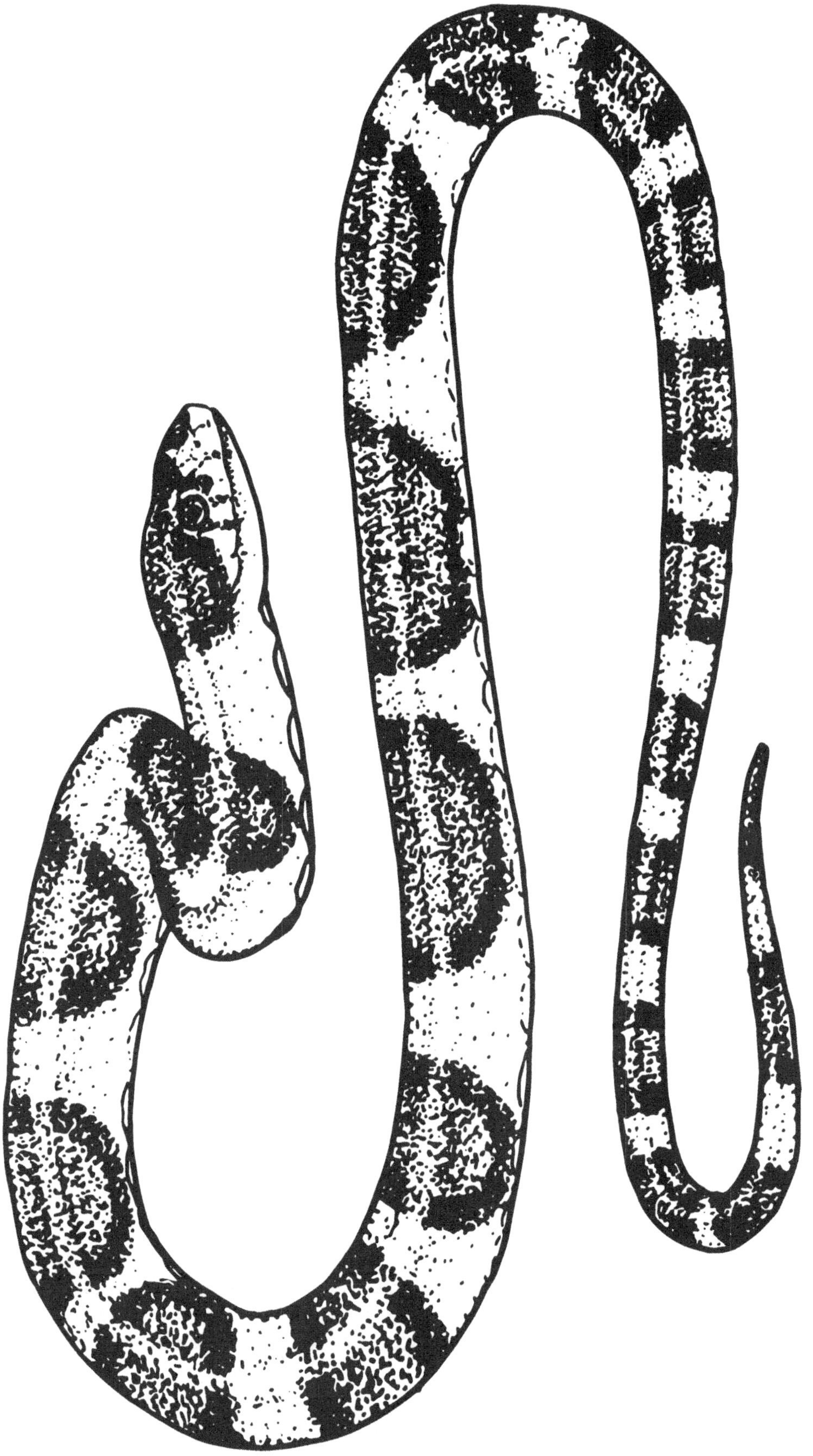

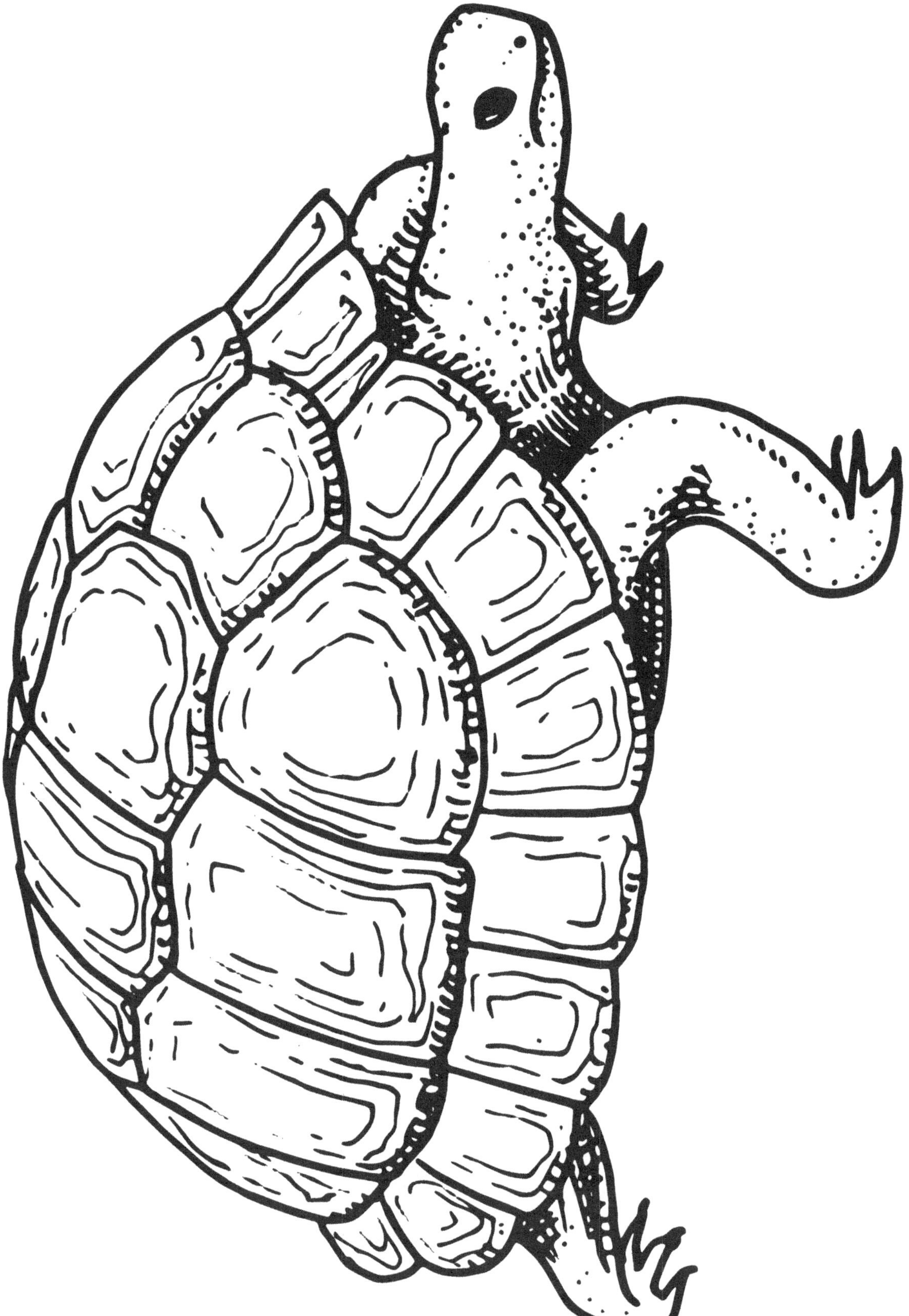

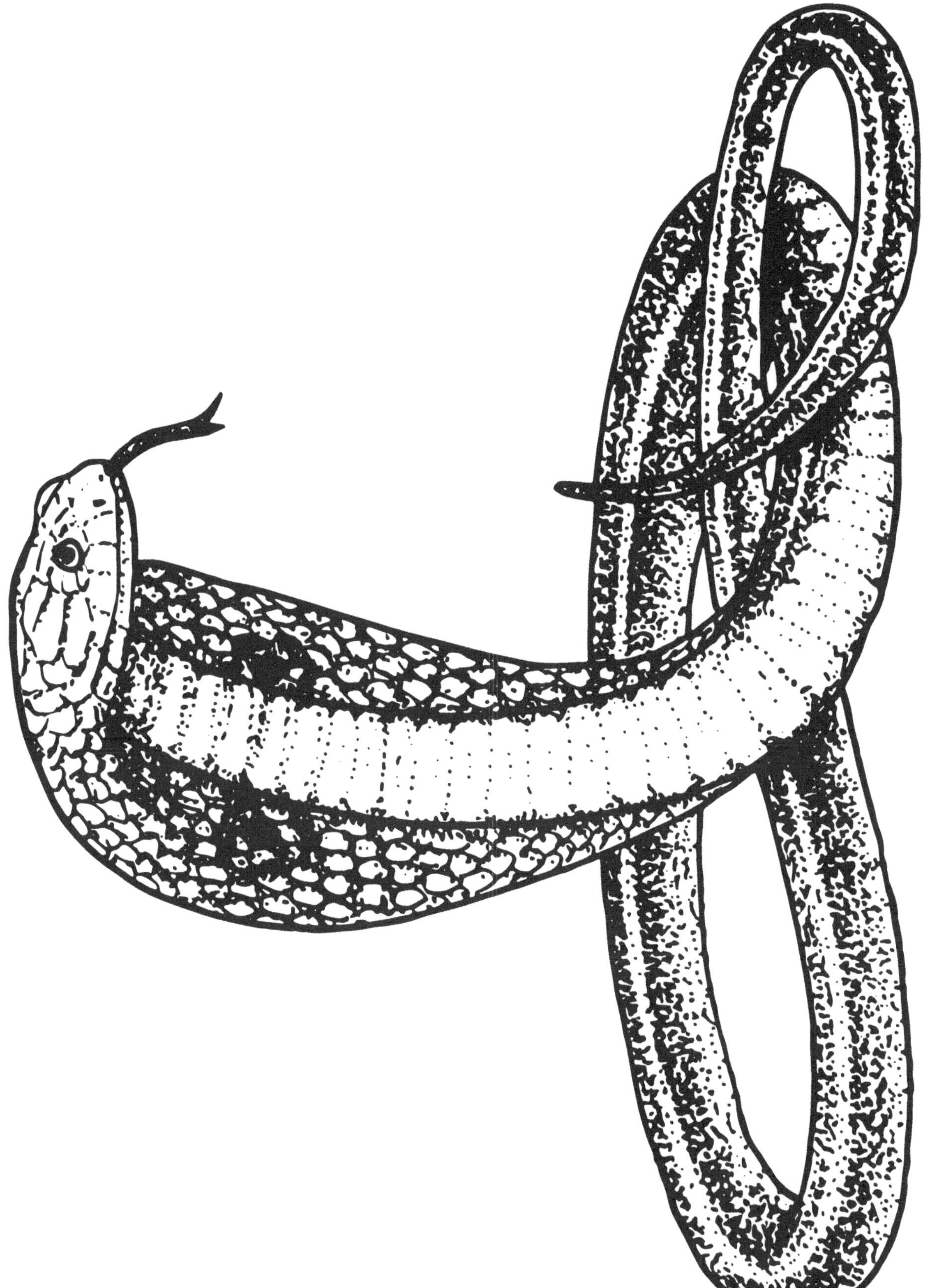

This is a Bleed Through Page If You Are Using a Colouring Marker or Pen!

Find Other Great Titles By searching for Bold Illustrations on Your Favorite Book Retailer

Amazon.Ca | Barnes & Noble (BN.Com) | Books A Million (BAM.Com)

Made in the USA
Coppell, TX
22 October 2021

64486082R00046